No. LVII.

THE MINOR DRAMA

A MORNING CALL.

An Original Comedietta,

IN ONE ACT.

By CHARLES DANCE, Esq.,

AUTHOR OF "THE COUNTRY SQUIRE," "THE DUSTMAN'S BELLE," "THE MAGIC HORN," "WHO SPEAKS FIRST," "A WONDERFUL WOMAN," "DELICATE GROUND, &c., &c., &c

FIRST PERFORMED AT THE

THEATRE ROYAL, DRURY LANE,

BY HER MAJESTY'S SERVANTS,

On Monday, March 17th, 1851.

NEW YORK:

SAMUEL FRENCH, PUBLISHER,

122 NASSAU STREET.

DRAMATIS PERSONÆ.

GENTLEMAN.

Sir Edward Ardent..............................MR. JAMES ANDERSON.

LADY.

Mrs. Chillingtone....................................MRS. NISBETT.

A MORNING CALL.

SCENE.

A well-furnished drawing-room in MRS. CHILLINGTONE'S *house in the country*—MRS. C. *discovered working—Her work-table being near the fire—Snow storm without, which gradually ceases, and discloses a winter landscape.*

Mrs. C. People declare that everything in England is changed; I wonder what they would say to this specimen of a fine old English winter. The snow falls thickly enough to chill a lover; if, indeed, such an animal ever existed, except in the imagination of some dreamy poet. Talking of lovers, let me look at this note once again.

[*Putting down her work—taking up note and reading.*

"My dear Fanny,—

"I am sorry, for my own sake, that you declined to join "the large and merry party who are now staying here—not "so for your's—for there is a plot against you, and I am for- "tunately enabled to put you on your guard. Never mind "how I came to know it—it is enough that I did not par- "ticularly listen, only—when gentlemen are on visits at "country houses, they should ascertain exactly how their "rooms are situated, before they talk too loud. I need not "tell you, that it is well known that your early marriage "was a forced one. It is, now, equally a matter of notori- "ety that you mistrust the whole of the opposite, or, as you "call them, the 'opposing' sex, and that you have resolved "never to marry again. I quite differ from you on this "point, but never mind that—the subject was canvassed, a "heavy wager was laid that you would break your resolu- "tion within a week; and your appointed conqueror is Sir "Edward Ardent. As your house is but a few miles from "this, and as he has but little time to spare, if he really "means to win, I should not wonder if he were to rlde over "this very day, and make a morning call." *(Speaking.)* In- "deed! "He has the reputation of making great profes- "sions to every handsome woman he meets, without coming "to the point with any; but you know him better than I do." *(Speaking.)* Yes, I know him. "He is a good-looking, "good-for-nothing, fascinating fellow, and that's the truth, "I only wish he would make love to me." *(Speaking.)* No doubt, my dear. "However, I believe he is in very safe "hands with you." *(Speaking.* So do I.*)* "Take care of "yourself, and make an example of him for the sake of our "sex in general, and of yours, dear Fanny, in particular.

CHARLOTTE."

So, my gentleman, I am to surrender in less than a week, am I? the fortress must be badly defended indeed, that can't hold out for that time. It isn't worth thinking of, and I don't care a pin about it; but the man's impudence is almost provoking, and, little as it signifies, I delare I can hardly help wishing that this renowned general would commence his attack, that I may silence his batteries, and send him about his business. *(Shivering.)* Ugh! how cold it is, a little bit of a skirmish might warm one, for positively the fire wont. [*Rings the bell, and pokes the fire.*

Enter SIR EDWARD ARDENT, *in a hunting dress.*

Sir E. *(Aside.)* The snow puts an extinguisher on our hunting to-day, and some amusement I must have, so I have come to try if I can win the widow, *and* my bet. *(She rings a second time.)* She rings again—what does she want, I wonder?

Mrs. C. Coals.

Sir E. Ma'am?

Mrs. C Coals.

Sir E. Coals?

Mrs C. *(Looking up.)* Dear me, Sir Edward Ardent I declare, I beg your pardon, I took you for my servant.

Sir E. Would that you would *keep* me for your servant!

Mrs. C. What wages do you ask?
Sir E. I'll serve you for love.
Mrs. C. You'll never get paid.
Sir E. Engage me, and I'll take my chance
Mrs. C. You have great confidence.
Sir E. Not too much.
Mrs. C. Yes you have—in *yourself*, I mean.
Sir E. Never mind, enagage me?
Mrs. C. I've heard a bad character of you from your last place.
Sir E. Indeed! from whom?
Mrs. C. From your mistress, to be sure.
Sir E. What mistress?
Mrs. C. Have you so many?
Sir E. None! but I seek one, and *that* one——
Mrs. C. Will have a remarkably troublesome servant.
Sir E. Well, if I am not allowed to finish a sentence——
Mrs. C. My very good friend, when you are talking with a lady, think yourself remarkably well off if you are allowed to *begin* a sentence.
Sir E. I am quite aware that ladies——
Mrs C. Are very unreasonable on that subject—generally speaking, they are—I am an exception. You wish to say something?
Sir E. I do—something very——
Mrs C. Stop a minute—you shall have every chance—sit down and warm yourself, while I work. *(he sits.)* when you feel inclined to speak—speak., and I won't interrupt me.
Sir E. (rises.) I cannot sit—I am too much agitated. *(paces the stage.)*
Mrs C. Well, whatever you do, don't walk about, for that is unbearable.
Sir E. I don't know what to do.
Mrs C. Poor man! then I'll tell you—fetch the scuttle, and put on some coals.
Sir E. Hadn't I better ring for your servant?
Mrs C. Certainly not! when I rung for him you answered the bell, and not only that, but you applied for the place.
Sir E. He is shaking the snow off my coat.
Mrs C. An additional reason for your doing his work,

and so let me see how well you can do it. *(he fetches the scuttle, which he carries with both hands.)* Very well, very well—upon my word I think you have been in service before; there, don't spill them, or I shall have to send you about your business.

Sir E. (stopping.) Mrs. Chillingtone, listen to me, I am serious——

Mrs C. Not with the coal-scuttle in your hand, usrely.

Sir E. It is very hard that you will turn every thing I say into ridicule: however, in the hope that artificial warmth may thaw the natural iciness of your disposition, I will make up the fire before I unburthen my mind.

Mrs C. Stop! I have had hundreds of serious speeches made to me, but it just occurs to me that I never heard one from a man with a scuttle full of coals. Speak just as you are, scuttle and all.

Sir E. No! indeed, I shall not.

Mrs C. Now, do, pray; you can't think how well you look.

Sir E. You must excuse me. I certainly cannot see why a man who feels earnestly should not express himself earnestly at any moment; neither do I see that the ebullition of a genuine feeling is rendered less worthy of attention by the accidental circumstance of his having a coal-scuttle in his hand; but *(throwing some coals on.)* you have chosen to point attention to the fact, and possibly *(throwing more.)* there *may* be some degree of ridicule attached to it. Therefore, although I burn ro speak *(he looks at her, she is looking another way.)* I say, Mrs. Chillingtone, although I burn to speak *(throwing all that remains on.)*

Mrs. C. Don't smother the fire on any account.

Sir E. (putting down the scuttle, and pacing the stage—aside.) Her cool indifference is past belief. I'm not used to be treated in such a way by woman, and yet there *are* moments when I fancy that she is listening more than she pretends to be.

Mrs C. Are you speaking to me, Sir Edward? because I don't hear one word you say.

Sir E. I was talking to myself.

Mrs C. And there is no better way of ensuring an attentive listener.

Sir E. Thank you, Madam.

Mrs C. (rising and coming forward.) You and I have known one another a long time; why say "Madam?" it sounds very formal.

Sir E. Does it, does it? (*aside.*) She thaws—by Jupiter, she thaws! (*aloud, and earnestly.*) Does it?

Mrs C. Does it, does it, does it? Why, yes, it does—and what then?

Sir E. (aside.) Down to the freezing point again. I'll pretend to go, and try what that will do.

Mrs C. I haven't had the speech yet; when are you going to begin?

Sir E. Some other time; I think I hear a carriage. (*going.*)

Mrs C. I hear none, but if any body should call, I can say "not at home."

Sir E. (aside.) Oh, ho, my lady! *(returning.)* Well, since you will say "not at home"——

Mrs. C. I didn't say I *would*—I only said I *could.*

Sir E. Mrs. Chillingtone, good morning. (*going.)*

Mrs C. Nonsense! stay where you are, you restless man.

Sir E. You're very kind, but I must go. (*goes to door, which he opens and holds in hand, standing half-in and half-out.)*

Mrs C. Where to?

Sir E. I don't know; but good bye.

Mrs C. Till when, then?

Sir E. (aside.) She says "till when?" It's my private opinion she wishes me to stay.

Mrs C. Till when?

Sir E. Till to-morrow. *(aside.)* One day's absence will bring her to her senses. (*going.)*

Mrs C. Not to-morrow, you cruel man.

Sir E. (shutting door and returning.) Ah! you wish me not to go to-day.

Mrs C. I don't wish you not to go to-day—I only wish you not to come to-morrow.

Sir E. Shall you be out?

Mrs C. No, I shall be at home; but I shan't want you.

Sir E. (*aside.)* It's nothing to me; but as sure as fate, there's a man in the case—it's nothing to me, I say, but I don't like it. (*aloud.*) "You shan't *want* me," Mrs. Chillingtone—"you shan't want me?" that is, don't misunderstand me, I don't mean to say it's likely you would want me, but when you say you don't want me, it seems as much as to say you don't wish for me; of course, I don't mean to say it's likely you would wish for me, but when you say, or *if* you say, you don't wish for me, it's *almost* as much as to say that you wish me away; I say *almost*, I don't say *quite*.

Mrs. C. But I do; you have been a long time arriving at a conclusion, but the curious part of the business is that you have arrived at the right one.

Sir E. After such a declaration, it would be folly in me to say another word.

Mrs. C. A declaration? good gracious! Who has made a declaration? I heard none.

Sir E. This is trifling; I say it would be folly in me to say another word.

Mrs. C. So it would, so it would; but you'll say it for all that.

Sir E. Well, I believe I shall, in fact, I must; I have a question to ask you—a question, my dear Mrs. Chillingtone, to which I must entreat your most serious attention. (*she walks gently off to her own room.*) I will not add to your embarrassment by even looking at you while you answer it, contenting myself with merely begging that your answer may be a candid one. (*listens.*) Yes, cost what it may, a candid one. (*listens again.*) I pause for your assurance that it shall be a candid one. (*aside.*) She hesitates—she's lost.

Mrs. C. (*calling from within.*) Are you gone, Sir Edward?

Sir E. Gone, Mrs. Chillingtone? gone? Why *you* are gone.

Mrs. C. (*re-entering.*) Only for the moment. I went for my thimble.

Sir. E. Went for your thimble! (*aside.*) Women have always an excuse at the tips of their fingers. (*aloud.*) Only for a moment! Don't you know what Mrs. Haller says? "There are moments in which we live years."

Mrs. C. I must beg, Sir Edward, that you won't quote Mrs. Haller to me. I never associate with ladies of that description.

Sir E. (*aside.*) This is put on—she must be shamming, for she couldn't know that I was—how deceitful women are!

but I *will* go now. *(going to door.)* I positively will go. *(opens door, then stops—aloud.)* Surely you heard my question.

Mrs. C. Well, I fancied I heard you mumbling something.

Sir E. Mumbling! *(aside.)* Well, well, I'll bear it all—my turn *must* come. *(aloud.)* I asked you why you wished me away?

Mrs. C. What! to-morrow?

Sir E. Yes.

Mrs. C. Oh! because I expect somebody else.

Sir E. A man?

Mrs. C. Ah, that's the worst of it!

Sir E. A husband, perhaps?

Mrs. C. No, a simple man.

Sir E, The more simple, the more likely to become a husband.

Mrs C. That is the most natural thing you have said yet

Sir E. Why so.

Mrs. C. It's so rude.

Sir E. I didn't mean to be rude; make allowance for my feelings—I *feared* it was a husband.

Mrs. C You needed not have feared it. When you asked if it was a man that I expected, I said "that's the worst of it." I could not have said that, if it had been a husband.

Sir E. *Now,* who is rude? but I care nothing for the rudeness—I derive warmth and comfort from the openness of that assurance.

Mrs. C. (imitating his tone.) And I derive neither warmth nor comfort from the openness of that door! so I wish you would shut it.

Sir E. Oh, Mrs. Chillingtone, you are *too* cold.

Mrs. C. I told you so.

Sir E. (going towards door.) Be content; I am about to shut it once and for ever.

Mrs C. And when you have shut it, on which side of it do you propose to remain?

Sir E. Has the lovely Mrs. Chillingtone a choice upon the subject?

Mrs. C. The lovely Mrs. Chillingtone has *no* choice upon

the subject—but the lovely Mrs. Chillingtone, like the rest of her too fascinating sex, has considerable curiosity.

Sir E. Your wish shall be gratified—I remain on *this* side. (*comes in, having shut the door.*)

Mrs. C. I excuse the impertinence of that speech for the sake of its amusing vanity.

Sir E. (*aside.*) I'll let her go on—I'll let her go on—there *will* come a day of reckoning.

Mrs. C. Well, Sir?

Sir E. Well, Ma'am!

Mrs. C. Oh, nonsense! you mustn't repeat my words—you must say something; suppose this were a play, you couldn't come into a room where a lady was, shut the door, and not speak.

Sir E. Perhaps you will be good enough to furnish the plot of the play.

Mrs. C. I fancy it would be more in my way to act it; however, I'll try my hand. I must begin, I believe, with the stage directions.

Sir E. If you please.

Mrs C. Well—"The stage represents a drawing-room in Mrs. Chillingtone's country house—a large party are assembled at another country house, a few miles off."

Sir E. What, on the stage?

Mrs C. No, no! that is only for *your* information, to help you what to say; now, don't interrupt me, and don't speak till I tell you. "Mrs. C. has been strongly pressed to join the party at her neighbor's house; but, knowing herself to be rather an attractive person, and knowing that men, always more or less silly about women, think it behoves them to make especfal donkies of themselves when on a visit it a country house, she has declined. "One of the gentlemen———"

Sir E. Donkies!

Mrs C. "Sir Edward Ardent, by name"—(I told you not to interrnpt me, and you see what you have got by it) —"thinks proper to ride over to Mrs. Chillingtone's under pretence of a "morning call," although it is very evident to her, that he has some other object lurking behind.

Sir E. How does she know that?

Mrs C. I'm writing a play, and I'm not bound to tell more than I like.

Sir E. But I have to speak presently, and I want information.

Mrs C. You shall have more than you want. "Sir Ed ward, like hundreds of other moderately good-looking men, has been humoured by sundry weak women until he fancies himself irresistible."

Sir E. *(aside)* He may prove so yet.

Mrs C. "And, taking advantage of a previous acquaintance with Mrs. C. to deprive her of her privilege of saying "not at home," he breaks through the ordinary rules of society—enters—her room without being announced—and"—

Sir E. Stay! I can explain all.

Mrs C. Can you? that is just what I want; but don't be in a hurry—pull that couch this way. *(he pulls a couch to the centre of the stage.)* "Mrs. Chillingtone, though astonished at his coolness, takes her seat on one side of the couch *(she sits)* and motions Sir Edward to occupy the other" *(he prepares to do so—when he is nearly seated, Mrs. C. puts her hand under his arm and causes him to rise again)* "He has *almost* done so when he suddenly recollects that he has omitted to bow on accepting the invitation." *(he bows to her)* "Having supplied the omission, he takes his seat, and Mrs. Chillingtone waits patiently for the promised explanation of his extraordinary conduct."

Sir E. I can give it in five words.

Mrs C. Not less?

Sir E. Yes, in three—"I love you!"

Mrs C. Stay a minute—let me clearly understand. Are you carrying on the little drama I began, or are you, Sir Edward Ardent, *Bart.*, in your own proper person, addressing yourself to me—Fanny Chillingtone, widow?

Sir E. I hope you don't take me for an actor.

Mrs C. Well, in love affairs, there is not much difference between a man on and a man off the stage—one is a professional actor, and the other an actor of professions.

Sir E. You think, then, that truth has no part in love affairs?

Mrs C. Oh, yes it has, I wish it hadn't.

Sir E. Why so?

Mrs C. Because it always comes to late.

Sir E. Always?

Mrs C. I speak from my own experience.

Sir E. You have never tried but once.

Mrs C. And have no inclination to try again.

Sir E. You think all men alike, then?

Mrs C. Yes, in their disposition to deceive women.

Sir E. May there not be *one* exception?

Mrs C There may; but it must be a golden one.

Sir E. Come, I have gained a step at last—you admit there may be one exception—I trust before the week is out to prove myself that one.

Mrs C. A week? that is a very short time.

Sir E. If I fail to convince you of my sincerity in a week—

Mrs C. You'll own yourself beaten—and pay——

Sir E. *(rising)* Mrs. Chillingtone!

Mrs C. Sit down, Sir Edward—and pay your court to some one else.

Sir E. (aside) What a fool I am, I had nearly betrayed myself! *(aloud)* Where failure would be death, I will think of nothing but success.

Mrs C. What a charming speech! many men have offered to live for me, and I have refused them—you propose to die for me—now if I thought I could depend upon you——

Sir E. *(aside.)* Confound your impudence! but I'll be even with you yet. *(Aloud.)* You may—indeed, you may.

Mrs C. As you have allowed yourself so short time for your conquest—hadn't you better begin?

Sir E. If you please. I confess, and indeed, I think you must feel, that I start under some disadvantage. I have proclaimed that I love you—I have played out, as it were, my thirteenth trump, and am now dependent upon you to bring in my strong suit.

Mrs C. Your position is even more awkward than you think—if I play your cards as well as my own, you must be "dumby."

Sir E. Play them on *any* terms, I am content—it makes us partners.

Mrs. C. Was ever knave more civil to a queen? But look you, Sir Knave, a husband who must not open his mouth——

Sir E. Can never contradict his wife.

Mrs C. True! but a wife who is compelled to talk for two——

Sir E. Is confirmed, without a struggle, in her sex's dearest privilege.

Mrs C. *(aside)* I could almost like him for his impertinence.

Sir E. *(after a pause)* I'd give the world to know your thoughts.

Mrs C. You shall know them for nothing ; I was thinking which I should prefer—a deaf husband or a dumb one.

Sir E. If you allude to me——

Mrs C But I do not.

Sir E. I only said "if." If you allude to me, I will be dumb, *not* deaf.

Mrs C Why not deaf?

Sir E. I could not bear to *see* you speak, and thirst to hear the liquid music of your voice.

Mrs. C. It's very kind of you to think me so charming and I dare say you're quite right ; but if you were dumb you could not tell me so.

Sir E. What matter? I could find other means to make you know it—I could lie at your feet the live-long day, like a pet dog, with happy eyes to see you, with greedy ears to hear you, and express, by mute devotion, that deep affection which, at last, no tongue, however eloquent, could tell.

Mrs C. *(aside)* Hang the fellow, how pleasant he talks!

Sir E. *(aside)* She's touched.

Mrs C. There is only one thing, I fear, Sir Edward.

Sir E. *(earnestly)* Say what it is? It ceases with the utterance.

Mrs C. If you were to become my pet dog——

Sir E. Yes?

Mrs C. I'm afraid you would expect me to wash and comb you every day. *(laughs at him, rises, and walks about.)*

Sir E. *(rising, and paces the stage)* Really, Mrs. Chillingtone—this indifference—I wish you wouldn't laugh—this indifference—now, pray don't laugh—this indifference to one who—oh, well, if you are determined to laugh, it's useless to attempt opening one's mouth.

Mrs C. There, there, I won't laugh any more *(sits down)* I'm dumb, and will only express by mute devotion, that (what is it? oh!) that deep affection which no tongue, however eloquent, can tell.

Sir E. I should be sorry, Mrs. Chillingtone, to charge

you with affectation, but this indifference is unnatural, it is unworthy of your sex, and, allow me to add, *unlike* your sex. *(aside.)* I'll try if I can make her jealous; *(aloud.)* for I don't hesitate to tell you that it has been my fate to make an impression upon the fairer portion of the creation, which, in point of numbers, I believe to be quite unusual; it is not one, two, ten, or twenty only, that I might have married, had I but held my little finger up. I havn't a particle of vanity in my composition; but common sense tells us there must be something about me to account for the very marked preference shewn me by the ladies.

Mrs C. Don't mistake me! I always listen with pleasure when my own praises are sounded, though I seldom take the trouble to enquire to what regiment the trumpeter belongs; you may go on.

Sir E. It is now some three years since first I met you; on that occasion it was my good fortune to dance with you —shall I ever forget that dance? no! to my dying day the very tune will haunt me —it was a polka!

Mrs. C. No such thing; it was a quadrille.

Sir E. You're right, it was. I said it but to try you.

Mrs C. *(aside)* I wish I had held my tongue.

Sir E. *(aside)* I didn't remember a bit about it; but that's nothing. *(aloud)* You are quite aware that I never even hinted to you the passion with which you then inspired me.

Mrs C. *(aside)* Now, *is* he going to have the effrontery to pretend that he has been in love with me all this time?

Sir E. No, like the gentle Viola, I "let concealment feed on my damask cheek."

Mrs C. While you yourself fed, I suppose, on your damask table-cloth.

Sir E. Is this a moment for levity? I ask you, *is* this a moment for levity? but I am rightly served—women have adored me by dozens, and I have sported with their feelings, I have slighted them, poor dears! but, at length, to avenge their sufferings, you step forward as their appointed champion, and, I, in turn, am doomed to the bitter pangs of unrequited affection. Oh, Mrs. Chillingtone, may you be saved from such a fate! You have many admirers (not so many, I dare say, as I have) but a great many—you snub them all, but beware ! the time and the man may come, and you may meet in our sex, the avenger I have found in yours.

Mrs C. There's no great danger.

Sir E. I don't know that ; love delights in tormenting —women are weak creatures, men are full of deceit.

Mrs C. You must be going to publish a copy-book.

Sir E. Extremes frequently meet ; she who begins by hating, often ends by loving ; some day you may be addressed by one whom, like myself for instance, at first slight—he may be very good-looking, although you may think him plain —his figure may be nearly faultless, and you see nothing in it—his conversation, winning to all other ears, may fall unheeded upon yours—nay, even his voice, to many soft and sweet, may sound to you harsh and discordant. And yet this man shall bend your stubborn spirit—and how ? I grieve to say by flattery ; he shall tell you you've a pretty foot.

Mrs C. Oh, Sir Edward !

Sir E. And praise, as indeed he may with truth, your dancing ; he shall talk of the beauty of your figure——

Mrs C. Oh, Sir Edward !

Sir E. And compare it, to its advantage, with the classic forms of old ; he shall discourse of your brilliant wit——

Mrs C. Oh, Sir Edward ! you'll prevent me from speaking at all.

Sir E. And, having thus fixed your attention, and secured your silence, he shall tell you that your voice is "linked sweetness, long drawn out," that your face [*Mrs C. leans back, and throws a white handkerchief over her head*]—but here description fails me—not because, as a proof of your unequalled modesty, you have concealed it—but because language offers not the means to do it justice. He no doubt will feel the same difficulty, and passing to your hand, which perhaps he may perceive, as I do now, for once without a glove, he shall, transported by his feelings, venture to take it within his, and finding no resistance, even to press it to his lips —then will you be convinced of the depth of his devotion, then, on a sudden, will the change take place—then will his figure in an instant become good, his face handsome, his conversation brilliant, and his voice musical—then : but possibly I offend you—I will release your hand [*he lets it go, it falls by her side.*] How is this ? Is she ill ? No ; slightly overcome—it's only another victory, gained a little sooner than I expected. Edward Ardent, what the devil *is* there in you, that no woman on earth can resist you? I *must* look at her [*pulls the handkerchief from her face*] Fast asleep, by all that's horrible! [*walks up and down, much excited*] It's enough to drive one mad—downright, stark, staring, raving mad—but she wakes.

Mrs C. [*who has only pretended to be asleep, pretending to awake*] What's o'clock? Oh, what a dreadful noise you make. I was having such a nice nap.

Sir E. And charming dreams, no douht?

Mrs C. Yes, till just this minute. I dreamt that a nice, gentlemany man was saying all sorts of captivating things to me.

Sir E. *(aside)* Indeed! *(aloud)* You *do* care about the creatures then?

Mrs C. Not a bit; but you know how absurd dreams are.

Sir E. Very likely. "A nice, gentlemany man was saying all sorts of captivating things to you."

Mrs C. When suddenly he turned into a monkey, and grinned and chattered most repulsively. At length the monster darted at my hand; I fancied he was going to bite it, and———I suppose that awoke me.

Sir E. Others can awake from dreams as well as you. Madam, good morning. *(going.)*

Mrs C. Where is the man going to?

Sir E. "The man!" the monster, you mean.

Mrs C. Well, the monster.

Sir E. To the Zoological- gardens.

[*Exit.*

Mrs C. He is actually gone; and some women would say "I have lost him for ever." I knowing a little more of the world—allow him five minutes, at the outside, to return.

Re-enter SIR EDWARD.

I have been too liberal. [*to* Sir Edward.] What! won't the Zoologicals have you? have they too many specimens already?

Sir E. No, but they won't receive me without a certificate from you.

Mrs C. Of what, pray?

Sir E. That I have been your pet monkey.

Mrs C. You grow insulting, Sir: and I shall leave the room. [*going.*]

Sir E. Nay, that is more my duty.

Mrs C. So I think; but until you do, I shall.

[*Exit, slamming the door.*

Sir E. Oh! very well, Ma'am. (*he watches her out.*) Go? I should think so. Go? I should like to know who would stay (*sits down.*)

Re-enter Mrs. CHILLINGTONE.

Mrs. C. Not gone yet, Sir Edward?

Sir E. Returned so soon, Mrs. Chillingtone?

Mrs. C. Having a right to suppose the house clear, it surely was not very wonderful that I should return to my own drawing-room.

Sir E. Oh, I'm gone. I merely came back to look for my little dog. [*whistles.*] Trim, Trim, Trim. (*whistles again.*) Where on earth has the dog got to? Trim, Trim, Trim.

Mrs. C. That was not your real excuse, Sir, so don't condescend to deceit.

Sir E. You are right, it was not. I returned to prove that I was not quite a monster, and to take my leave somewhat less abruptly

Mrs. C. Why go at all?

Sir E. Do you wish me to remain on your account?

Mrs. C. Oh dear, no; on your own. After being so excessively warm, it might be dangerous to rush into this frosty air. (*laughs at him.*) Sudden changes sometimes produce astonishing effects.

Sir E. (*aside.*) Sudden changes! "I thank thee, Jew, for teaching me that word." I'll try a sudden change. (*aloud.*) I've no objection to staying an hour or two, as you seem to wish it. (*goes to fire place—draws chair, and seats himself with his back to her.*) Have you got such a thing as a newspaper?

Mrs. C. A newspaper, Sir Edward? A newspaper, in my company!

Sir E. Why not? You went to sleep in mine.

Mrs. C. I was not asleep, Sir.

Sir E. Oh! you were only pretending?

Mrs. C. That was all. I heard every word of the nonsense you talked.

Sir E. Ah! you may well call it nonsense. What rubbish one does talk to women—doesn't one? And the best of it is, they believe it—poor things!

Mrs. C. "Poor things," Sir Edward! "poor things!" You don't flatter yourself that I believed what you were saying; although it was easy to see that you meant every word.

Sir E. Have you seen the poker anywhere?

Mrs. C. The poker!

Sir E. What *can* there be in women that, although quick to detect us when we flatter others, they invariably gorge the bait themselves?

Mrs. C. *I* gorge the bait, Sir Edward!—I!

Sir E. How can my remarks apply to you? You are a professed man-hater.

Mrs. C. I have never said anything of the sort.

Sir E. Well, you have given out that you mean never to marry again!

Mrs. C. I don't know that I have gone so far as *that*; but that has nothing to do with it. You have been for the last twenty minutes making me professions of admiration and attachment. I need hardly to tell you that they were perfectly indifferent to me; but the extraordinary alteration in your tone and manner gives me a right to have this question answered—did you mean them?

Sir E. (laughing.) No.

Mrs. C. Were you attempting to make a fool of me?

Sir E. (laughing.) Yes.

Mrs. C. (aside.) This is a little too much.—*(aloud.)* Look you, Sir Edward Ardent, your assumed coldness——

Sir E. And your assumed excitement——

Mrs. C. I don't say that it *is* altogether assumed.

Sir E. You're annoyed, then?

Mrs. C. Not the least annoyed; but I'm excessively provoked at the deception you have practised. But it was *not* a deception—I won't admit that it was a deception. You were quite sincere.

Sir E. Not I.

Mrs. C. You admire me beyond any woman you ever saw.

Sir E. Now, pray don't talk nonsense.

Mrs. C. You do—and you love me to distraction

Sir E. Don't I look as if I did ?

Mrs. C. I don't care for that. You love me to distraction—and if you don't, you ought. And whether you do or not, after what you have said, you are bound to marry me if I insist upon it ; and rather than you should go away and have the impertinence to brag to your male friends that you have had the best of it, I *do* insist upon it. So now, Sir, marry me, and then we shall *see* who has the best of it.

Sir E. (altering his tone.) Are you serious ?

Mrs C. Perfectly.

Sir E. (rising, and coming forward.) Then for once, Mrs. Chillingtone, *I* am serious. You had a perfect right to determine not to marry again ; but the pains you took to make that determination public, looked like a studied insult to us bachelors. At all events, it was so considered ; and, at a special meeting duly convened, it was voted that you should be made to break your resolution. I have succeeded in conquering your boasted aversion to mankind—but there, I regret to say, the task assigned me ends. In taking my leave, I will not affect to deny that I admire you ; or that I felt much—perhaps, too much—of what I said ; but all personal considerations must bend before a sense of public duty. It became necessary to read you a great moral lesson ; and—with a the sternness of a judge who carries out the wholesome rigours of the law, but with the feelings of a gentleman who grieves to pain a lady—I have read it. *(bows, and is going.)*

Mrs. C Stay, Sir Edward—*(he stops and turns—(aside)* Flesh and bood can't bear this. *(aloud)* Stay for a moment, and ask yourself your true position. Victor as you think yourself, it's not a proud one. A set of men combine to form a plan against one poor weak woman : you are selected as their scape-goat : if you fail, they're ready with their jeers,—if you succeed, the victory is theirs—the odium yours.

Sir E. (aside) I'm dreadfully afraid that's true

Mrs. C. (aside.) Now for it *(aloud.)* And you have succeeded but too well : my pride is humbled,—the advantages which you possess of face and figure——

Sir E. [aside.] Oho !

Mrs. C. Those brilliant powers of conversation which Nature has given you, and which you so fatally can use, have brought me to your feet—and now you propose to leave me.

Sir E. How is this? Can it be that you really love me.

Mrs. C. Can it be that you know yourself, and doubt it? Oh, Sir Edward, would that the choice of my appointed conqueror had fallen on one less fascinating—or that your pride had been content to feed on victories past, nor claimed another female slave to chain to your triumphant chariot-wheels! [*much moved.*] But thus to conquer, and thus cruelly to leave, is but a wanton exercise of power, and may be likened to that of the fowler, who shoots the bird he cares not to preserve, for the mere pleasure of seeing the hapless creature die! [*Weeps.*

Sir E. (*aside.*) Die? D——n it, she musn't die! I've gone too far. (*aloud, and with a patronising air.*) No, no, my dear Mrs. Chillingtone—I have no pleasure in anything of the sort, I assure you. Calm yourself, I entreat you. I'm sure you won't attribute it to anything in the shape of vanity, when I say that it is evident I have been a little more fascinating than I intended. I meant to win your consent, certainly—and I have won it; but thinking—pardon me—that you were *rather* heartless (at least, so I understood you understand,) I never dreamt—(don't you see?)—that I should touch your *heart.* It only shows that one never knows one's own powers: however, though thoughtless, and perhaps wild, I trust that I am still a gentleman; (*aside.*) how deuced well she looks through her tears! (*aloud.*) and rather than see a lady suffer on my account—(*aside, having looked at her again.*) oh, by George! a man might do a great deal worse—(*aloud.*) I offer you, this time in all sincerity, my hand and fortune.

Mrs. C. Sir Edward Ardent knows but little of the woman whom he honours with his pity, if he supposes she would wed a king upon such terms. It is my duty, however, to thank you for your generous offer—the more generous because affection has no share in it.

Sir E. Now, Mrs. Chillingtone, upon my word, you must not say that. I assure you, I'm extremely fond of you—I was afraid I was—I mean, thought I was: but this last half hour has convinced me.

Mrs. C. It will take longer to convince me.

Sir E. Time is nothing—sincerity, everything. I am the most devoted of your slaves.

Mrs. C. I'm sorry to hear it: the best slaves make the worst masters.

Sir E. I'll promise anything.

Mrs. C. So will a servant seeking a situation—so will a candidate for a seat in Parliament—and so, no doubt, would a king, were the office elective,

Sir E. How can *you* hope to escape a risk which is common to all? Any man may break his word.

Mrs. C. And where women are concerned, most men do.

Sir E. Men, not gentlemen.

Mrs. C. Am I to understand that you are a gentleman, and not a man?

Sir E. At present, think of me only as a lover.

Mrs. C. Which I presume, means neither.

Sir E. It means either, both, or neither—at your bidding; I am the slave of the lamp.

Mrs. C. Say rather of the ring.

Sir E. Good; I am the slave of the ring, ready to obey you in all things. I entreat you make trial of your power.

Mrs C. You shall be indulged. Fetch my bonnet and shawl; *(he goes for them)* and while you are about it, bring your own hat. *(he returns with them.)* Now put that on. *(he is about to put on his hat.)* No, no, put on my bonnet.

Sir E. Not your bonuet!

Mrs C. Yes, and shawl. *(he puts on the bonnet and shawl.)* Good, now give me your hat. *(he gives it to her.)*

Sir E. What next, I wonder?

Mrs C. Now, Sir, according to your own modest account, ladies have been making love to you all your life. I am curious to see how a lady looks when she so demeans herself; *(putting on his hat.)* fancy me the fascinating man, which you evidently fancy yourself. Down on your knees, and——I leave the rest to you.

Sir E. Well, if I must—there. *(kneels.)* Hear me, then you captivating tyrant, while I own that I love you, and ask, in all humility, for a return.

Mrs C. (aside.) I have him down at last, and there I,ll keep him. I fear I care too much about him, and love is sweet; but to an insulted woman revenge is sweeter.

Sir E. I entreat you to relieve me from a position which is not only painful, but extremely inconvenient. Do you love me ?

Mrs C. What if I do ? You are aware that all personal considetations must bend before a sense of public duty. It is necessary to read you a great moral lesson.

Sir E. You do not love me, then ?

Mrs C. (*takihg of the hat, and throwing it away.*) No ; I was shamming.

Sir E. (*rising, and throwing away the bonnet and shawl.*) So was I.

Mrs C. Your assertion comes a little too late, Sir. What would you have me infer from your having been on your knees to me ?

Sir E. That I have dusted them, and want a clothes-brush.

Srs C. Indeed !—my servant will furnish you with one as you go out.

Sir E. Very well, Madam—I understand your hint : but remember, I go to bear witness to my friends that you accepted me, and I declined,—I'm bound to speak the truth.

Mrs C. Ay, and the whole truth ; you will therefore be pleased to add, that subsequently *I* declined the honour *you* proposed.

Sir E. I'm afraid that will make me look ridiculous.

Mrs C. Not more than you do now, I think.

Sir E. There is one way to make it bearable.

Mrs C. And that is——

Sir E. Union is strength ; let us be married and share the ridicule between us.

Mrs C. A very handsome offer ; half your ridicule is to be my marriage settlement.

Sir E. Half all I possess on earth—nay the whole. I get the better half again if I get you.

Mrs C. But will a general, so celebrated in the field of love, be content to renounce all future conquests ?

Sir E. Let him but win this final battle, and he will. You shall be his Waterloo—in conquering you he masters all the world—for you, henceforth, are all the world to him.

Mrs C. It seems that, like schoolboys, we have played till we have become in earnest. Well, (*giving him her hand.*) be it so ; and let us hope that our friends—though they may laugh at us, and welcome—will enjoy, each evening, some pleasing reminiscence of "A Morning Call."

www.ingramcontent.com/pod-product-compliance
Lightning Source LLC
LaVergne TN
LVHW020633110826
845149LV00004B/1165

* 9 7 8 1 4 1 8 1 9 1 4 7 4 *